Around Grays

IN OLD PHOTOGRAPHS

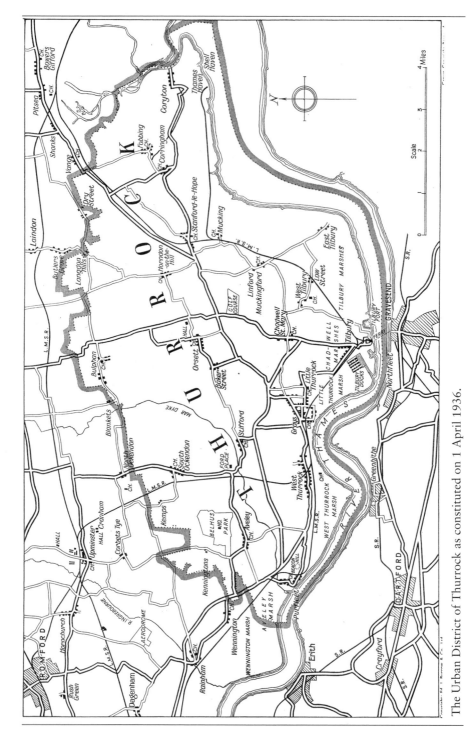

The Urban District of Thurrock as constituted on 1 April 1936.

2

Around Grays

IN OLD PHOTOGRAPHS

BRIAN EVANS

Budding BOOKS

This book was first published in 1994 by
Sutton Publishing Limited · Phoenix Mill
Thrupp · Stroud · Gloucestershire· GL5 2BU

This edition first published in 2001 by
Budding Books, an imprint of
Sutton Publishing Limited

Reprinted in 2002

British Library Cataloguing in Publication Data.
A catalogue record for this book is available from
the British Library.

ISBN 1-84015-257-5

Typeset in 9/10 Sabon.
Typesetting and origination by
Sutton Publishing Limited.
Printed in Great Britain by
J.H. Haynes & Co. Ltd, Sparkford.

Contents

Established in Victoria's reign, Westwood and Sons was one of the well-known and popular stores flourishing in Grays main shopping area during the 1920s and '30s.

The immaculately dressed shop windows at Westwood's.

Introduction

Created in 1936, the Urban District of Thurrock included a score of communities around Grays, which is situated between the River Thames, then a busy shipping highway, and the uplands to the north. A wealth of history can be traced by the determined researcher, as the area was sometimes at the forefront of national events, but more often in the shadows of local struggles for power and influence. There is a diversity of interests: industry and farming, docks, lost harbours and quiet inland resorts. Each town or village had its own story, whether it had been left behind by the changing times or newly created by the needs of manufacturing.

In prehistoric times, the mammoth, bison and hyena roamed by the riverside swamps or trampled through the wooded uplands of the region. Artefacts from the Stone, Bronze and Iron Ages are buried in the local soil, and evidence of Roman farms, burial grounds and favoured sites (with a good water supply, and so on) is also to be found in the locality. It was settlers in the early Middle Ages, however, who made the greatest impact. Many of the local place-names are derived from the Saxon, and one of the most important archaeological investigations of a Saxon site has been carried out at Mucking. Until these discoveries were made in the 1960s the area was little known. Extensive excavations, spanning thirteen years, increased knowledge of the Saxon world to an incredible extent. One thousand graves and two hundred Saxon huts, plus thousands of pieces of pottery, were unearthed.

A bronze-bound wooden bucket, from the grave of a male Saxon at Mucking.

SECTION ONE

Grays Town

A port in medieval times, the town of Grays Thurrock takes the second part of its name from the Saxon word for the bottom of a boat, where mud collects. This was an allusion to its location on a bend of the Thames where silt gathers. The first part of the name (the part now commonly used for the town), comes from Henry de Grai of Graye, Normandy, who was granted the town in 1195. The busy little port expanded during the nineteenth and early twentieth century, no doubt stimulated by the arrival of the railway in 1854.

The bottom of the old High Street, 1912. Note the weatherboarding. On the left is the White Hart and the house on the right is the former Hope and Anchor. Being close to the quays, both inns were the haunt of sailors.

The junction of London Road and Orsett Road, before the First World War.

A view of the High Street, north of the railway, *c.* 1910. There are still private houses in the middle distance (right) of which only the front garden walls and trees can be seen, but this photograph shows how the street had developed as a shopping centre.

There are still many local shops but national chain stores are beginning to appear, *c.* 1910. Note the Lipton's delivery cart.

Looking from the police station across to the east side of the High Street, 1910. The Queen's Hotel on the left always had the appearance of a military establishment, removed from Woolwich or Aldershot and set down here.

Cyclists, pedestrians and a horse-drawn cart give Grays the air of a market town, belied only by the newer bank and commercial buildings on the right, 1910.

The Queen's Mansions was an old public hall before it was taken over by the Grays Co-operative Society in 1922.

A branch of Burton the men's tailors had opened in the High Street by 1936, indicating renewed confidence in Grays as a shopping centre, after the economic depression of the late 1920s and early 1930s. The pale façade of Burton's can be seen here, centre left.

Police Station, Orsett Road, Grays.

The new police station was built in the early 1930s. It gave a certain dignity to the town, in keeping with its growth as an important administrative centre for the area.

PC 750 Frank Talbot is seen at the rear of the building, 1940. He was a typical policeman of the old school and was fond of a joke. The police at that time were paid a very low wage, but they remained loyal to the force and had a knowledge of dealing with people which was partly instinctive and partly learned from older PCs. Soon after this, more scientific training was given and a new breed emerged.

The fire station (right) opened in Orsett Road in 1893. It was demolished in the mid-1970s, in line with the trend of moving fire stations to the edge of towns.

FREE LIBRARY, GRAYS.

Grays Library (right). The library dates from 1903 and cost £3,000, which was given by Andrew Carnegie. The plot on which it was built was donated by Charles Seabrooke JP. The houses beyond were gradually replaced by shops.

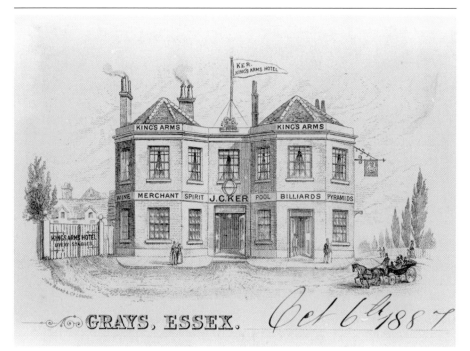

A billhead from the King's Arms, *c.* 1865. It was described as a 'family and commercial hotel and posting house', and at this time John Ker had taken over from John Arthur Cuming.

A view from the old market-place by Grays parish church, 1908. The old part of the High Street is in the centre of the photograph, with the King's Arms to the left and the Rising Sun to the right. At that time eight public houses could be visited within a short distance of this spot.

HORNCASTLES

CASH OR TERMS

TELEPHONE:
TILBURY 511

ESTABLISHED
1845

FURNISHING, CARPETS & LINOS,
76 & 78, HIGH STREET.

IRONMONGERY,
CHINA & GLASS,
1 & 3, NEW ROAD.

GRAYS, ESSEX.

Furniture Repaired and Re-polished; Bedding Cleaned and Re-made; Linos. and Carpets laid; Blinds, Curtains, Loose Covers, &c. made and fitted.

An advert for Horncastles furnishing business shows their two shops. On the left are the rebuilt premises facing the old market square and on the right is the shop at 1 and 3 New Road.

Horncastles New Road and High Street premises, 1898.

A crowd of curious onlookers by the church of St Peter and St Paul, 1908.

The entrance into New Road in the 1930s. This road had gradually grown into a lively shopping centre, with firms such as Frank West, Noads, Lanhan & Pennington and the Grays Building Society.

A busy day in New Road, 1930s.

Joyes' exciting sale has lured a large crowd, mainly women and children, to the town's only department store at the time. No doubt the discounts, and prizes offered in a competition, created extra interest. The firm was situated at 4 and 6 New Road.

Mr Skinsley of Crabbe and Skinsley, hauliers in Grays in the 1920s, is seen outside the stables in Rosebery Road. A Harris Coaches garage later occupied this site.

Two views of the Dutch House in Old High Street, which was pulled down in 1950. Part of the structure dated back to the seventeenth century.

SECTION TWO

Leisure and

Entertainment

Simpler pleasures entertained the people of the Grays district in the earlier part of the century. But horizons were expanding and the cinema and radio (then known as the wireless) were both soon to fill the minds of local people with more sophisticated ideas.

M. Cockley's stall with its display of fruit and other goodies at Gray's Recreation Ground, *c.* 1919. The boy in front can't believe his eyes.

Contrasts: (left) a path in Hangman's Wood, summer 1910, and (right) the winter beauty of Grays Park in 1920, providing recreational walks to occupy scarce leisure time.

Grays Park benefited from the elaborate planting of shrubs and bedding plants, which were the pride and joy of municipal open spaces from Victorian days up to the 1960s. It is pictured in around 1919.

In the 1920s and '30s, brick shelters, pavilions and public toilets were added so that a whole day could be spent in the park. Very often bands and entertainers performed in a specially fenced-off area around a bandstand. In 1936 Thurrock UDC took over twenty-nine parks and recreation grounds.

The Empire Theatre, Grays, seen in the early 1930s, was built in 1910. At first it showed silent films, but after 1915 these were supplemented by live music-hall entertainment. Many celebrated artistes appeared here, not least Marie Lloyd in 1916. The Empire closed in 1942 and after the war was used, with little alteration, as a greengrocer's shop.

A delightful shot of The Royal Pierrot company, dressed for a performance at the Ambrose Market, Grays, 1904.

Isa Bernard, the much idolized star of the Royal Pierrots, 1904.

A local band, 24 May 1919.

The Co-operettes concert party, *c*. 1926. These Co-op employees performed before a variety of enthusiastic audiences around this period.

The ICC cricket team from the Grays area, 1938 season.

A function at the Tilbury Hotel, 1936. Built as part of the Tilbury Docks development, the facilities were of a high standard. Just eight years after this photograph was taken the hotel was destroyed by incendiary bombs dropped from a German warplane.

SECTION THREE

Residential

Residential houses in the Grays district once came in every shape and size, from the impressive Belhus Mansion of the Barrett-Lennard family, with its multitude of servants and large surrounding estate, to rows of primitive, thatched rural cottages. The mansion has been demolished and part of the estate built on, but one group of cottages, surprisingly located in Orsett Road, Grays, rather than on the rural fringe, survived into the twentieth century.

Polwicks: a solidly built farmhouse of the seventeenth century, with a later extension of a type which was common in the northern and eastern agricultural districts around Grays.

Sherfield Road, 1906. The coming of large industrial concerns created a growing demand for housing in the town. This row of Victorian houses leads down to the riverside area.

Whitehall Road was also built to house the new workers, and was part of the north-eastern growth of Grays towards Chadwell St Mary.

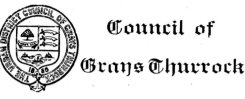

The Council of Urban District Grays Thurrock

No. 343

ENGINEER AND SURVEYOR'S OFFICE,
HIGH STREET,
GRAYS, *17th May* 192*8*

Certificate of Completion of Dwelling Houses.

I hereby Certify than I have examined *one* bungalow house in *Windsor Avenue*

within the Urban District of Grays Thurrock, erected by *Messrs Brown Bros* for *Mrs Robson*

and find the same to be completed in accordance with the bye-laws

relating to New Streets and Buildings, in force within the said

'District, and to be in every respect fit for human habitation.

Engineer and Surveyor.

A Grays UDC certificate of completion for a Windsor Avenue house, 1928. The town was now expanding north towards Stifford. Each of the old local councils tried to keep control of building standards in the face of rapidly rising demand.

The Dell was a rather exclusive corner of Grays, created out of an old chalk pit. The house itself was also known as the Dell and was built for Alfred Russell Wallace, a naturalist who lived there until 1876. His ideas formed the background to Darwin's theory of evolution but Wallace received none of the credit.

Grays Hall Hill, 1911. Its impressive houses were spacious enough for the large families of the time.

Palmer's Avenue was laid out around 1890 to bypass the old route out of town, which had a difficult right-hand bend, and to create a more impressive entrance to the town from the east.

The bottom of Bridge Road, lined with basic Victorian cottages, many of them two-up, two-down. The house behind the garden on the right was grander and became a doctor's house and surgery. Beyond its gate pillars is the entrance to Grove Road.

No. 1258

ORSETT RURAL DISTRICT COUNCIL.

PALMER'S AVENUE, GRAYS.

No. of Plan _3129_

CERTIFICATE OF COMPLETION.

To _Mr. R. E. Watts._

Southend Rd. Stanford le Hope

Bungalow....

This is to Certify that I have examined the House.... erected by

M _yourself._

situate _No. 8. St James Aces._

Stanford le Hope.

for which Plans were duly deposited and approved by the Council, on the
_19th_ day of _March._ 19_31._ , and that the same has (or have)
been carried out as far as can be inspected in accordance with such Plans
and the Byelaws of the Council.

Dated this _6th_ day of _October._ 19_33._

G. F. Andrews

Engineer & Surveyor.

N.B.—Any person occupying any house before having received the Surveyor's Certificate
is liable to prosecution.

This is not the Certificate required under the Public Health (Water) Act, 1878, Sec. 6.

A Stanford le Hope certificate of completion, 1933. Some of the villages around Grays
had been expanding slowly since the advent of the railway but development accelerated
after the First World War.

SECTION FOUR

First World War

During the war women joined the industrial workforce in many important areas and replaced the men who had been conscripted. Key male workers were kept at their posts, together with older men, to help with industrial training, where their assistance was vital to the war effort.

These men seem proud of their contribution to the munitions drive. They are Kynoch's 'Cordite' B Shift, 1917.

Before the war, but training for the real thing: soldiers at Orsett Camp.

Grays Company, Chelmsford Regiment, trained and ready for action, 1915.

Thames Board Mills female workers with some of the men exempt from military duties.

The *Warspite* moored off Grays, 1931. During the war she had been the cruiser HMS *Hermione*. In 1929, after a £20,000 refit, she was adapted as a nautical training school for 275 boys of good character.

The War Memorial at the junction of Orsett Road, High Street and London Road was unveiled on 6 March 1921. It replaced the horse-trough and public lavatory which had originally stood in front of the old police station, seen here on the left.

SECTION FIVE

Education

A local feature from the late nineteenth to the early twentieth century was the positioning of naval training ships offshore. The *Cornwall*, *Goliath*, *Exmouth*, *Warspite* and *Shaftesbury* were all anchored here at different times, and the lads were frequently to be seen ashore, engaged in various dry land activities such as sport. A charity school was founded in the town in 1706. This eventually became Palmer's Grammar School, which has occupied two sites in Chadwell Road. In the nineteenth century other schools were opened in the High Street, New Road, Bradleigh Avenue, Dell Road, Arthur Street and Bridge Road, and Roman Catholic schools were established in church buildings in Argent Street and East Thurrock Road.

The *Goliath* on fire: she burnt at her moorings on 22 December 1875. A full account of the tragedy was written by J.R. Fenn, the schoolmaster on board, and published in 1876. Built in 1835 she had been used for training at Grays since 1870, accommodating 520 boys and officers.

The *Exmouth*: two vessels of this name were moored off Grays over a period of more than sixty years. The first, an old wooden three-decker, was established by the Metropolitan Asylums Board to replace *Goliath* in 1876. The second, modelled on her predecessor but with a steel hull, came in 1905 and left in 1939. Seven hundred boys were trained on board for the navy.

Bridge Road Boarding School dates from 1898. It was an upper-standard school for 600 senior pupils taken from existing local schools. Photographed in 1906, it was extended in the same year to accommodate 840 pupils.

The old buildings of Palmer's School, 1909. Some of the female pupils are benefiting from the fresh air in this elevated part of the town. The school had moved to this site in 1874. From 1876 both boys and girls were educated here but in different parts of the building.

The old library, Grays, was in use from 1903 to 1972, and is remembered with affection by many. Seen here to the left, a lane leads up to the old chalk pit (along which a railway track originally ran down to Grays wharf).

The John Henry Burrows Intermediate School, Hathaway Road, 1936. It had opened in 1931 and was designed to accommodate 360 pupils.

SECTION SIX

The Beach

An artificial beach of fine sand, together with a raised walk, seats and shelters, was opened in August 1906. This deliberate creation of a seaside atmosphere at Grays took advantage of the fine outlook on the river at this point. Apart from distant views of Kent there was a great deal of shipping to be seen making its way to the Port of London. Grays port was also a lively scene at the height of its activity; it was home to the largest known sailing-barge fleet, which was owned by E.J. and W. Goldsmith.

An Edwardian idyll: children on the beach, Grays, 1906. In the background are barges and the training ship *Exmouth*.

There appears to be a children's outing in progress in this view of the beach, *c.* 1908. A tent has been erected at the back.

Children enjoying themselves on the sands and in the water, *c.* 1908. Note the saplings and the refreshment facilities along the promenade at the rear.

The bathing pond, which was next to the beach, 1914. It was used a great deal especially at holiday times, but the swans were probably only visitors.

Grays beach, 1920s. Barges can be seen at the wharves in the distance.

The promenade, pictured in 1909, was a favourite spot for the older generation of Grays, particularly for those who had been connected with maritime occupations. The view of the Kent bank, which was just visible between a half and three-quarters of a mile away, and the higher ground behind was excellent.

SECTION SEVEN

Industrial History

In 1841 Grays parish alone contained chalk pits covering some 30 acres. Chalk-quarrying on a grand scale had begun by 1688. William Palmer, Lord of the Manor, leased a chalk pit, known as the Slade, and two limekilns at Grays. This pit was operating in 1787 and was in competition with the nearby pit owned by Zachariah Button and situated west of Hogg Lane. A later entrepreneur, John Meeson, and his partners operated many local chalkworks, including the Titan pit behind the library site. Incredibly this fairly small pit was said to have provided a great proportion of the chalk whiting used by the English building trade, and it was even being exported to America in 1852. By 1866 two of Meeson's pits, taken over by the reconstituted Grays Chalk Quarry Company, were connected by a tunnel under Hogg Lane, and in 1876 they were said to be a vital part of the town's economy. Beginning in 1789, brickmaking in Grays soon became the biggest industry. In the nineteenth century large parts of the town were given over to the works. These areas are now Bridge Road to York Road and Arthur Street, Kent Road and Salisbury Road. In addition, railway lines snaked across the yards on their way down to the wharves, where the bricks were packed into barges and dispatched to London. In 1808 some five hundred men produced bricks for the construction of the defence line of Martello towers along the south-east coast. These two industries alone figured in the prosperity of the port and wharves, though Grays coastal trade is recorded as early as 1228.

Samuel Whitbread's quarry at Purfleet with its early horse-drawn-wagon railway, which connected the quarry with the Thames and other parts of the works, 1807. The Whitbread family owned the Manor of West Thurrock from 1777 to 1920, largely controlling the development of Purfleet.

Diagrams of the construction and loading of the Purfleet quarry wagons, 1807. The Purfleet quarries had been in existence since the 1550s but declined and closed down in the 1840s.

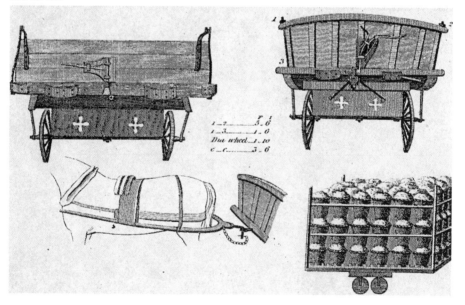

Isolated pinnacles of rock were left in the workings. These were all that was left of the original solid hill and Thameside cliffs. The quarry became a leisure resort with soft grass and plantations of abundant trees.

A typical scene along the Grays wharves, 1897. This barge is loaded with flour, and was the first delivery to be made to the wharf just purchased by the Grays Co-operative Society.

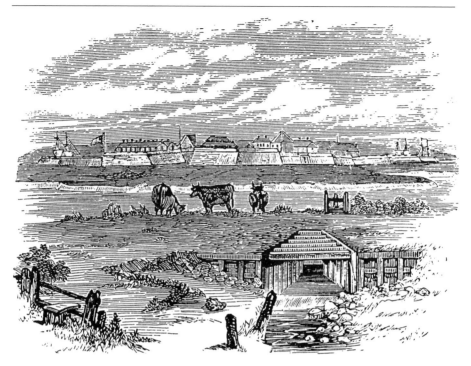

A view from the site of Daniel Defoe's tile works towards Tilbury Fort. Daniel Defoe, the famous writer, was first the secretary and then the owner of the works from 1695 to 1703.

Aveley Mill, with the miller and his family, May 1902. At one time almost every village had access to its own mill to grind the local corn. In addition there would usually be an associated bakery in the village street. This particular mill was dismantled in around 1916.

Purfleet from the Thames, 1810. Fishing was still a viable trade at that time; later the railways improved transportation, and importing catches from fishing centres further afield became a simple business.

The waterworks at Grays: testing the jet at the engine-house. The water flooding the chalk works in the mid-nineteenth century was put to good use by the proprietors of the Grays Chalk Quarry Company, when a separate firm, the South Essex Waterworks Company, was established to sell the commodity.

Seabrooke's Brewery, Grays, had a very efficient delivery fleet, so it is surprising that it ceased trading. Founded in around 1800, it was taken over by Charrington's in 1920.

An old submarine at Ward's Yard, Grays Wharf, waiting to be broken up, 1930.

Purfleet was chosen by the Anglo-American Company (now Esso) for its works. At first, crude oil was brought across the Atlantic in barrels loaded on barges towed by a larger ship.

A new crude-oil refinery was started at Thames Haven in 1922.

Two explosive places. Above, the entrance to Kynoch's works. The armament manufacturer purchased 200 acres of marsh in 1896. The works were closed and sold in 1919. In 1923 they were renamed Corytown (later Coryton) after the firm of Corys, and an oil refinery was set up here. Below, Purfleet Garrison. A large store of gunpowder was moved from Greenwich to this location in 1700 as it was safer to keep it away from large centres of population. Troops were stationed here to protect the stores.

SECTION EIGHT

North of Grays

North of Grays stretches a fertile farming area, which remained relatively unchanged from medieval to recent times. Saxon place-names proliferate in the villages, farmsteads and hamlets. Higher ground north of the town belies the accusation that Essex is a flat county and provides some very attractive views and wooded beauty spots.

The developing village of South Ockendon, *c.* 1910. Note the recent arrival of street lighting.

An engraving of Belhus from the late eighteenth century. This was the great house of the area and although the exterior was not a great feature the interiors were very fine. The original family after whom it was named came from Ramsden Bellhouse in Essex to settle here in about 1327. At the time of this picture the family in residence was the Barrett-Lennards, and not long before, Thomas had remodelled the house in Gothick style.

Belhus, 1910.

The contents of the house were dispersed in 1923. This photograph shows the south drawing room, as illustrated in the sale catalogue.

The dining room, 1923. The house was said to be haunted and sightings have been reported by many witnesses over the years – even a servants' cottage, Cherrytrees, had its ghost.

The Queen's bedroom, 1923. Elizabeth I is said to have slept in this room when she stopped at Belhus en route to Tilbury; there she reviewed the troops assembled to repel the Spanish Armada in 1588. In the sale of 1923 there was keen competition for items in this room – surprisingly, not for the bedstead but for two eighteenth-century mahogany bookcases, each of which made 305 guineas.

The Tapestry bedroom, with the 5 ft carved-oak canopy bedstead. The back has twelve panels and six apostolic figures in high relief, and the bedstead realized 97 guineas at the sale.

The hall. In its latter days (1900–23) the house suffered a severe rat problem – according to Mrs Duligal, a servant in the house during the First World War, many of the rodents were as big as cats. Sir Thomas Barrett-Lennard would not allow them to be killed and so all food had to be put under cover; otherwise it would all have been eaten up.

Modern development in Stifford Road, Aveley, in the 1920s contrasted with the rural surroundings.

St Michael's Church, Aveley. The oldest part is the early twelfth-century nave, but there are Roman bricks in the ragstone and flint walls. The bricks must have come from a Roman building in the neighbourhood, but details are not known.

A mixed herd of cattle outside the farmhouse at Bretts Farm, Aveley, *c.* 1930. A milk-float (behind) and a van advertise D.P. Watts' pure new milk.

Outside the Carriage House at Bretts Farm, *c.* 1910. Holding the horse is Harry Smith and behind, leaning on the wall, is Norman Percy Smith.

The binder at work in the fields at Bretts Farm, *c.* 1910. Norman Percy Smith is in the centre of the group.

The barn at Bretts Farm, with Norman Percy Smith in the centre (right), *c.* 1910. Many of the traditional methods of farming were still used at that time, but mechanization and government controls were just around the corner.

Bulphan Rectory, 1870s. The Church of St Mary provided a focal point for the rather scattered village. Many roads in the area have sudden sharp bends – perhaps a relic of the days when much of the fen was flooded and evasive action was called for.

Looking down the hill from Horndon village, 1920s. The trees meeting over the roadway indicate a traffic-free Essex.

A view up the hill. This road connected Horndon with Hornchurch and Ilford in pre-Roman days, and the 'horn' part of the name may refer to pagan worship at all of these sites.

The Bell Inn, Horndon, June 1929. It has fifteenth-century timber framing, and stage-coaches used to stop here.

The Church of St Peter and St Paul, Horndon, 1921. Beneath its shingled broach spire are carved faces. Other features are Roman bricks in the walls and a carving of a grotesque face, known as the Horndon Beauty, on the east wall of the chancel.

High Street, Horndon, 1904. The village is now a conservation area.

The comparatively modern church of St Mary, Langdon Hills, 1908. Nearby is a local beauty spot with excellent views. An older church of All Saints, lower down the hill, has a chancel and nave walls built of sixteenth-century bricks, but there are indications of a much earlier building.

The old post office, Langdon Hills, 1920. It was a boon to locals and tourists in what was then a fairly remote spot.

Orsett House and grounds. The house was built by Captain Bonham and dates from 1740. It is a fine three-storey brick residence and at one time it was used as a school. The rood screen in the church is connected with one of the Captain's descendents, Admiral Charles Bonham.

Orsett's seventeenth-century windmill, painted in 1905. Only the base now remains. The village, once the principal administrative centre for the area, is scattered.

A quiet day in Hall Lane, Orsett, 1919.

Attractive vernacular buildings in the High Road, Orsett, at the beginning of this century.

A rear view of Orsett Church, showing the two chancels and the railed, conical-topped tomb outside, 1870s.

A drawing of Orsett House in the 1870s, showing the Georgian features. Several attractive Venetian windows also adorn the building. The house is surrounded by trees and is connected with the Whitmore family, who became Lords of the Manor through a debt of honour. In addition, Sir Francis was Lord Lieutenant of Essex around the time of the Second World War.

The Old Pot Shop at the Orsett Show, c. 1909. The show began in 1841, and became a very important annual event in this area.

Pigg's bakery's new delivery vehicle, *c.* 1920. Pigg's was the first bakery locally to deliver bread by motor vehicle. The combustion engine was beginning to shatter the quiet of the villages around Grays at this time, though bread carts continued to be horse drawn in many areas long after the introduction of the motor vehicle. There was even a revival of horse-drawn transport for milk and bread delivery to save petrol during the Second World War.

South Ockendon Church and Green at the centre of the village, *c*. 1920.

Looking up the High Street, South Ockendon, 1910.

The smock mill, South Ockendon, was built in about 1828 and is pictured in around 1963. This overlooked a few remains of the old hall (the moat, bridge and part of a gatehouse), but it gradually fell to pieces.

St Nicholas' Church, South Ockendon, 1870s. Inside are several medieval masons' marks and a monument to Sir Richard Saltonstall, who was Lord Mayor of London in Elizabethan times.

A general view of North Stifford with the church to the left and Stifford Lodge, a Georgian residence, to the right. A fine avenue leads the eye towards the village.

J. W. PIGG & SONS, Ltd.,

Grocery, Corn & Provision Stores & Steam Bakery,

Central Stores, Socketts Heath, Grays

WILLIAM STREET, GRAYS, & ORSETT

Telephone — · — TILBURY 1044

DELIVERIES DAILY TO—

Aveley	Horndon-on-the-Hill	Stifford
Benfleet	Laindon	Thundersley
Bulphan	Leigh	Thurrock, West
Chadwell-St.-Mary	Linford	Thurrock, Little
Corbets Tey	Ockendon,Nth.& Sth.	Tilbury Docks
Corringham	Orsett	Tilbury, East
Dunton	Orsett Heath	Tilbury, West
Fobbing	Pitsea	Upminster
Grays	Purfleet	Vange
Hadleigh	Southend	Westcliff
Hornchurch	Stanford-le-Hope	

Pigg's has been one of the best-known businesses in the Grays area. Originating in Orsett this bakery and provision store gave its name to Pigg's Corner, north of Grays. Incredibly the bakery was still using this Victorian-style advertisement in magazines in 1942.

An old cottage in North Stifford, 1870s.

North Stifford Rectory, 1870s. This was once home to William Palin, the author of a two-volume historical study of the district, published between 1871 and 1872 and the source of some of the illustrations for this volume.

East of Grays

To the outsider, the people who lived on the marshes in the east were a different race. In more primitive times it is a wonder that anyone survived here. Marshmen are recorded as taking as many as eight wives, though it seems that many of these women succumbed to the marsh ague from which apparently the native men were mostly immune. Many centuries before, the Saxons had a thriving community on the marsh, travelling by boat from area to area. Excavations at Mucking from the 1960s revealed the surprising richness of their existence.

A truly rural public house: The Blue Anchor, West Tilbury, 1920s. The motor car gives an indication of the road development to come, although this village has changed less than most.

St Mary's Church, Little Thurrock, was built in the Early English style and is pictured in 1908. The area of Little Thurrock which is nearest to Grays has more or less been annexed to the town. Even so, and in spite of several modern developments in parts of the parish, old nooks and crannies remain.

Little Thurrock Wesleyan Chapel at the beginning of the century. It was built in a style which is common in the Grays area, and it is as if a little bit of Wales or the north of England had found its way south.

The entrance to Hangman's Wood, near Chadwell St Mary. This was a romantic bit of the parish in which the famed dene-holes lay; scientific debate about their origin has raged for over a century.

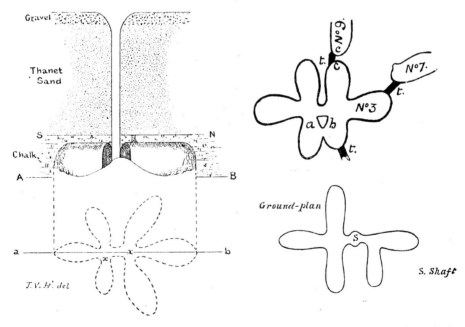

Sections and plans of the dene-holes. These double-trefoil-shaped pits may have had multiple uses in ancient economies: after the chalk had been dug out for liming the land the pits provided storage.

St Mary's Church, Chadwell St Mary, 1920s. The village lies on gravel beds and has been a popular settlement site since Roman times, as evidenced by the finding of Roman pottery and a hoard of coins.

River View, Chadwell St Mary, 1920s. The construction of modern houses has gradually turned this village into a considerable suburb.

River View, 1920s. Fine views of Tilbury Docks, which were actually built within the parish of Chadwell St Mary, may be gained from this higher ground (though not from this photograph).

Sleepers Farm, Chadwell. This is a late fifteenth-century timber-framed house. Many original timbers and evidence of jettying can be seen on this attractive building.

Two views of St Clere's Hall, Mucking. The house was originally known as New Jenkyns and was built in 1735 by James Adams, whose unusual tomb is at Stanford le Hope. The Georgian brick building is attached to a smaller older wing, and the castellated parapet also came later.

St Katherine's Church, East Tilbury, 1905. The medieval tower of this once very remote building is said to have been destroyed by the Dutch in the memorable year of 1667; the incident is described by Pepys in his diary.

This drawing of East Tilbury Church, with its view over the Thames, emphasizes how isolated it is. Colonel Gordon of Khartoum built the nearby Coalhouse Fort. Long afterwards, in 1917, the no. 2 Company of the London Electrical Engineers began to rebuild the tower in memory of the Coalhouse Fort soldiers (who had died in the First World War) and of Colonel Gordon. However, the work was never finished.

East Tilbury Place in a rural landscape, *c.* 1930.

Open for business: the post office and general stores, West Tilbury, *c.* 1930. In the eighteenth century this pleasant village shot to fame with the discovery of a mineral-water spring which had medicinal value. Attempts were made to develop the village into a spa, but they were probably hampered by its remoteness.

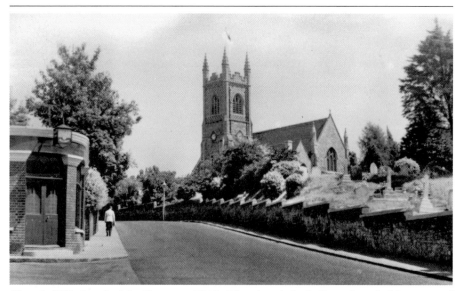

Church Hill, Stanford le Hope, *c.* 1912. The church is dedicated to St Margaret of Antioch and its structure incorporates Norman, Early English, Decorated and Perpendicular styles.

The War Memorial, High Street, Stanford le Hope, with the old cottages to the right, 1925. These had once been the Cock and Magpie inn, and they were nearly 300 years old when they were demolished in 1929. In the middle are the small premises of S. Cowell the ironmonger, and the handsome building to the left is a bank.

The High Street, Stanford le Hope, with the post office to the left, *c.* 1915. Stanford's most famous resident, the novelist Joseph Conrad, lived in a semi-detached house near here. He later moved to Ivy Walls in Billet Lane, where he lived from 1896 to 1898; it was during this time that *Nigger of the Narcissus* was published.

A sailing vessel entering the creek at Stanford le Hope, *c.* 1920.

The picturesque Bull Inn at Corringham was largely rebuilt in the seventeenth century, though a fifteenth-century cross-wing remains.

Corringham village retains many weather-boarded cottages.

Old Fobbing, across the creek, 1932. Smuggling features a great deal in stories about the village, as its main link with the outside world was once by water.

Fobbing village pond, 1920s.

St Michael's Church on the hill overlooking the old buildings that blend into the Fobbing landscape, 1911.

SECTION TEN

Tilbury

The deep-water docks at Tilbury were designed to cater for new trends in shipping goods around the world. Opened on 17 April 1886, the docks were constructed over four years at a cost of £3 million, about three times the original estimate. The docks company acquired about 460 acres of land, about 100 acres of which were occupied by the docks and adjacent facilities. The intention was that the largest ships of the time could enter and leave the docks at either low or high tide, thereby saving valuable time. To the north and east of this mighty undertaking a new community grew up, to run these facilities and the associated transport services. Very soon passenger liners were attracted by the convenience of the port and its good communication links with London.

Tilbury Fort at the end of the eighteenth century.

An old fireplace in the fort.

Tilbury Docks decorated for its opening, 1886.

A crowd in Dock Road, Tilbury, *c.* 1909. This suggests that there has been an open-air meeting.

Dock Road, late 1920s.

The school and chapel of Our Lady Star of the Sea. A busy community grew up around the docks, including a large Roman Catholic population.

Tilbury Hotel, on its little peninsula between the entrance to the docks and the steamship landing-stage, was part of the original docks scheme. It opened on 17 April 1886.

Tilbury Hotel was frequently used by travellers arriving and departing on the liners which sailed to every part of the world.

The view from the grounds. The hotel facilities were of a high standard: from the start it had electric lighting throughout and a regiment of porters, waiters, cooks, chambermaids and other staff. Unfortunately it was destroyed by bombs from a German plane in 1944.

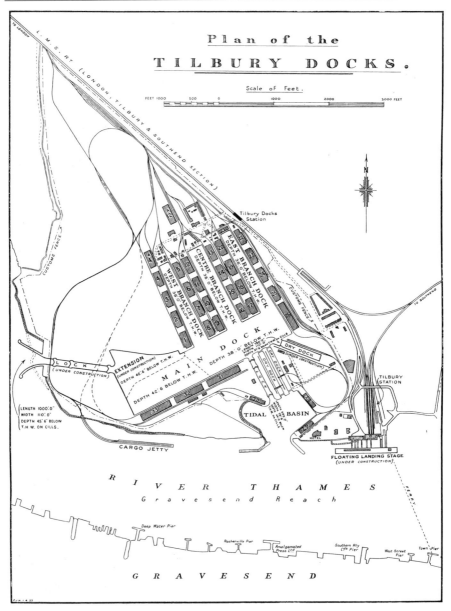

A plan of the docks at the time when the floating landing-stage was being constructed, 1927.

Tilbury and the Thames seen from Gravesend. Sailing-barges transported various cargoes which often included bricks, and the handling of the barges was a fine art, backed by generations of experience. Notice how low the Essex landscape lies.

The ferry and busy shipping-lanes at Tilbury, *c.* 1919.

The SS *Palembang* alongside a cargo wharf, 1925.

A dockside scene showing the manual handling of freight at the central dock, Tilbury, *c.* 1910.

The SS *Norman* in Tilbury Docks, 1925.

The *Viceroy of India* liner at Tilbury, 1931.

The SS *American Banker* entering Tilbury Docks, 1925.

This 'maid' steamer has run aground on the mud at Tilbury Docks, *c.* 1909.

The magnificent bulk of the mailship *Orotava* in the Thames, 1921. A small steam vessel is in the foreground and almost hidden under the side of the larger ship is a vessel which may be the ferry.

The SS *Naldera* being towed by a Sun Company tug, Tilbury Docks, 1925.

The SS *Branksome Hall* in Tilbury Docks. A Sun Company tug is in the foreground, 1925.

The Tilbury ferry *Catherine* in midstream, *c.* 1910.

The ferry *Edith*, 1905.

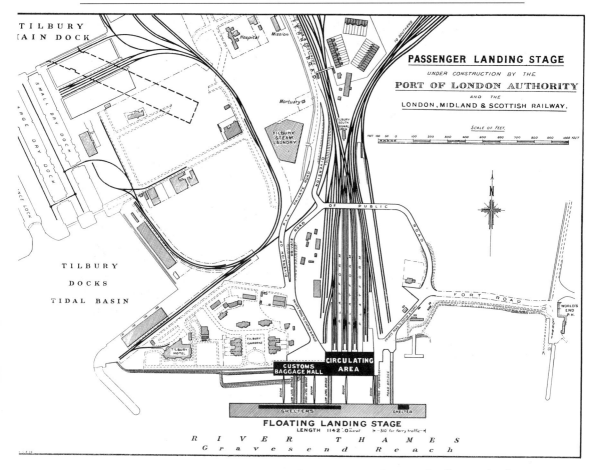

A map of the shipping-terminal area at Tilbury in 1927, showing the floating landing stage then under construction. The plan shows the location of other features of the terminal such as the hotel, gardens, hospital, mortuary, mission, and the Tilbury Steam Laundry.

An aerial view of this area shows a big liner at the mooring, the customs and baggage hall (bottom right), the Tilbury Hotel (centre) and shipping in the background.

An aerial view of the docks, looking south from above, 1920s. In the foreground are railway tracks and transit sheds, with the Tilbury Hotel, the Thames and Kent beyond.

Tilbury Docks. Seen here is the central branch dock, 1912.

The exterior of Tilbury station, and the pier, 1920s.

Looking along the new landing stage, which was built in 1927.

The Port of London customs and baggage hall, 1929. Beyond was the incredibly commodious station circulating area, which was meant to accommodate thousands of passengers en route between the ships and trains. It never quite reached the level of traffic it was planned for. In the latter days before its closure it resembled the *Marie Celeste* in its desertion.

The landing stage, 1930s. Its construction was a joint venture between the Port of London Authority and the London, Midland & Scottish Railway Company.

The P&O liner *Chusan* docks at Tilbury. Visible in front is the ferry, a familiar part of Tilbury river scenes.

West of Grays

This region includes South Stifford, West Thurrock and Purfleet, and it has been dominated in recent years by the extractive industries and a mixture of others along the Thames, such as detergent, margarine and packaging-board manufacture. Other changes include the rise of Lakeside Shopping Centre on the site of old cement works in the late 1980s, the building of the Dartford Tunnel, which was completed in 1963, and the complementary Queen Elizabeth II Bridge, constructed in 1990. Nevertheless, the area has rural and historic aspects.

The lighthouse on stilts at St Clement's Reach. It was one of several lighthouses set up in the mid-nineteenth century by Trinity House and placed on prominent bends in the Thames.

St Clement's, the pilgrim's church, stands near the shore, between the modern factories at West Thurrock. In medieval times it provided shelter and temporary rest for Canterbury pilgrims about to cross the river. Here they could pray for a safe passage.

Some trees and what appears to be a barn alleviate the ribbon development of London Road, West Thurrock, seen here before the First World War.

The dovecote at Hunt's Farm, West Thurrock, 1913. Doves provided substitute meat in the days when cattle had to be slaughtered at the beginning of winter, because crops had not been introduced and there was a lack of feed for them. This dates most of the surviving dovecotes to the sixteenth or seventeenth century. Hunt's Farm buildings have now been demolished.

The octagonal dovecote at High House, 1913. It has a turret and weathervane, and both the dovecote and High House date from the late seventeenth century. In the Essex vernacular dovecotes were known as 'duffus'.

Beacon Hill lighthouse, Purfleet, is pictured about ten years before its demolition in around 1920. Erected by Trinity House in 1829, it was used for experiments with various types of oils, lamps and reflectors to judge their effectiveness. The cliff on which it stood provided an energetic climb for Victorian tourists.

Entrance to the Botany Bay Gardens and rail station, Purfleet, *c.* 1906. Two tourists appear to be about to sample the pleasures of the gardens, which were located in the old chalkworks. They were open from 1859 until around 1909.

Railway staff at Purfleet station, *c.* 1906. It was popular in Victorian and Edwardian times for excursions. The iron bridge which led to the Botany Gardens is seen in the centre background.

London Road, Purfleet, 1920s. It was still quite rural but some development is visible.

The beach and Royal Hotel (right) at Purfleet.

A side view of the Royal Hotel. Before Purfleet became a resort the hotel was known as the Bricklayer's Arms. Later, as Wingate's Hotel, it was frequented by the Prince of Wales (who became Edward VII), Charles Parnell (president of the Nationalist Party) and Kitty O'Shea, who later became his wife.

A view from the Royal Hotel. In the background are the training ship *Cornwall* (right) and the coal-loading wharves.

Unlike the other training ships along this part of the Thames, the *Cornwall* was intended for truant boys. It was moored at Purfleet from 1868 to 1928.

Looking towards Beacon Hill, Purfleet, *c*. 1930.

Railway Terrace was part of Purfleet's intriguing Edwardian townscape. Many of the houses would have offered rooms to holidaymakers.

Jarrah Cottages and Digby's shop. Many of the postcards of Purfleet in the early decades of the twentieth century were produced by G.H. Digby and sold from his premises.

SECTION TWELVE

Transport

The far-sightedness of the London, Tilbury & Southend Railway Company (LT&SR) promoters in constructing their line along the Thames shore in this area in 1854 made this rather remote area more accessible, and in the long term this led to prosperity for the entrepreneurs who set up businesses and factories along this route. However, the short-term aim of the railway company was to capture some of the steamboat traffic on the Thames for which there was much competition. The great lure was the very popular resort of Rosherville Gardens, on the Kent bank of the river near Gravesend. Tourists would be ferried across the river from Tilbury. These links with Kent foreshadowed the post-Second World War construction of the Dartford Tunnel and later the Queen Elizabeth II Bridge. Together with the opening of the Channel Tunnel in 1994 these put the Thurrock district firmly on the European communication map.

Tilbury locomotive shed in the great days of steam, 1909. The engines were all immaculately turned out.

On the Grays–Upminster branch the token for single-track working was handed out and collected in by the signalmen. A token would be collected at one end of a stretch of single track and handed back at the other end, and was used as a safeguard to ensure that only one train entered the track at any one time, thereby avoiding collisions.

A train at Grays station in the early years of the century awaits the 'all clear to start' signal. The crossing gates on the High Street have already closed.

A panoramic view of Grays station from the footbridge, *c.* 1913.

Grays High Street, showing the level crossing, 1930s.

Ockendon station is the only intermediate destination between Upminster and Grays. A porter poses with his young child, *c.* 1905.

Notice the rough state of the platform surface, which would be unacceptable today on health and safety grounds. The platform awnings at the far end provide shelter only at the entrance and exit area.

The signal-box at Ockendon. The porter and his child again pose on the steps. He was probably breaking the strict disciplinary rules of the time. The long hours meant he may not have seen his child much at home, or perhaps his wife was working in the fields nearby to supplement the couple's income and he was looking after the child while at work. He would be relying no doubt on a telegraphic message from signal-boxes further down the line to warn him of any impending visits by his superiors.

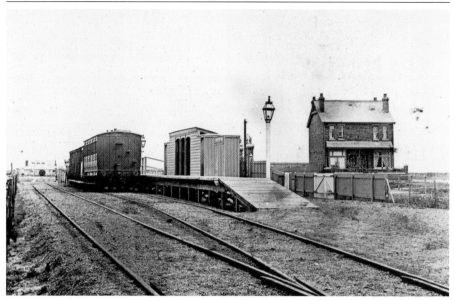

Corringham Light Railway at Coryton station. When Kynoch built its remote explosives factory out on the marshes in 1896 it was necessary to build a 2¾-mile rail line to link its workers and goods with the outside world. Beyond Corringham there was also a link with the LT&SR main line to transport goods.

A train near Corringham. Two locomotives were bought and named after company products – Cordite and Kynite. Six passengers a day originally made the 12-minute trip to the factory.

Sept. 10. 1951.
Daily Telegraph & Morning P

2½d RAILWAY STAYS ALOOF

◆

INDEPENDENT 3-MILE LINE

From Our SPECIAL CORRESPONDENT
CORYTON, Essex, Sunday.

Important people at Westminster may nationalise the railways, but a little thing like that does not bother the people here. The Coryton Non-Stop is a train which maintains an attitude of dignified aloofness to the whole unfortunate business.

In the nicest possible way it has gone on operating quite independently of British Railways, just as if nothing at all had happened. The fare is 2½d for a trip of just under three miles, but for regular travellers there is a weekly season at 1s 6d.

It should not be supposed that this is one of those miniature railways that are content to spend their lives on a narrow set of rails. Nothing but the best will do for the train that has been running regularly between Coryton and Corringham for the past half-century.

The gauge is of standard width. Even the Golden Arrow could spend a holiday running about on it.

Some features, however, are unusual. It is the engine-driver who issues your ticket and a few minutes later collects it.

LISTED IN BRADSHAW

The service is a public one and not without pride is attention drawn to the fact that it is tabled in Bradshaw. Yet there are only two journeys a day—one in each direction.

They meet the needs of some of the workers employed in constructing the Vacuum Oil Company's £10 million refinery at Coryton. But anybody else can join in.

It is perhaps fortunate that the line is not very long, for the scenery through which it passes can hardly be described as entrancing. It is a marshy area at the mouth of the Thames.

Even the tiny republic of Andorra would be impressed by the economy of manpower. One driver and one fireman are sufficient for the running of the railway, with two other men to keep an eye on the maintenance of the permanent way.

The only other member of the staff is a man who temporarily has to abandon other duties when the Coryton Non-Stop is actually carrying citizens He steps aboard as the brakeman, in conformity with the long-established safety regulation.

NO SIGNALS; NO SIGNALMEN

There are no signalmen, for a simple reason. There are no signals. This seems reasonable, because when there is only one train it cannot possibly bump into another.

In the long interval that occurs when the demands of " the travelling public " have been served, the engine, a pretty powerful one, discards its passenger coaches, substitutes wagons, and indulges in goods traffic.

If the Coryton Non-Stop were part of British Railways it would probably have had an imposing management organisation. Not being in that category, it is free to operate efficiently under one man, Mr. J. H. Freeman. The railway is one department of his many responsibilities.

He said to me with a smile: " It is something to be able to say to-day that you are a railway director. Regrettably, however, there are no board meetings, and I do not get any fees."

This 1951 article describes how the line stayed open while the new refinery was being built at what was by now called Coryton (formerly Kynochtown). However, the line finally closed the following year.

Seabrooke's Brewery delivery cart.

This was the first travelling shop used by the Grays Co-op. It served the early housing estates near Tilbury.

H. Crawshaw's bread delivery cart. Crawshaw changed jobs several times. He was a manager with the Co-op, which he left to take up a corner shop in William Street, Grays. Later he worked with Pigg's bakery.

A men's group outing in an Oxley coach, *c*. 1920.

An early motoring scene at South Stifford. Like many other garages this one developed from a cycle shop. E. North's shop was also a post office. These early garages at the side of the road were provided with fuel lines that swung out over the pavement to deliver the petrol.

The photographer Menlove rushed down to the beach to capture the arrival of this aircraft, which is thought to be a Maurice Farman seaplane of 1913 vintage. The Royal Naval Air Service at Felixstowe may have been trying out its capabilities.

Tilbury Riverside station, *c.* 1907. The generous platform space was provided to handle the expected great expansion in shipping traffic, which never completely materialized.

The interior of Tilbury Riverside station, 1920.

A smart turnout of staff grouped around Smith's bookstall at Tilbury Riverside station, *c.* 1910.

The worked-out top shelf of Grays chalk pit, 1951. It was in operation early this century, following the closure of the more prolific Purfleet deposits.

Acknowledgements

With thanks to: R.G. Ainslie for his assistance at a late stage; the *Daily Telegraph*; the Donald Maxwell family; the governors and trustees of the Passmore Edwards Museum for the use of illustrations; Peter Watt.